Monomaniac

Bates

ISBN: 978-1-913642-92-1

The author/s has asserted their right to be identified as the author of this Work in accordance with the Copyright, Designs and Patents Act 1988

Cover designed by Aaron Kent

Edited and typeset by Aaron Kent

Broken Sleep Books Ltd
Rhydwen,
Talgarreg,
SA44 4HB
Wales

Contents

Monomaniac

Liam Bates

'I began to miss light like it really is.'
   — Diane Arbus

Monolith

I notice it one morning, all
fifty feet, projecting from a square
of lawn at the far end of the garden.
Dad insists it's always been there:
he's sure we brought it with us
from the house where we used to live,
but I find this difficult to stomach,
me not seeing earlier, given its shadow
falls right across my window
for most of the day, its glassy grey
surface throwing light back, dazzling
prying neighbours and low-flying birds.
I would have noticed. Except growing
flush round its base is a daffodil rim
in uninterrupted spring bloom, which fits
with what Dad says or at least implies
the monolith didn't land or spring up
overnight. There's no chance these flowers
could survive that unscathed. I watch them,
a row of dancing stars like a halo
concussion round a cartoon's head.

Monograph

I'd like to leave my own body
of work beside these giants
of toilet wall artistry, to be
canon in a cubicle. Sitting
with the cistern to my spine
for the span of a history lesson
with the core question — how
best to render my message,
whether in words or in pictogram
with the rest of the phalluses.
Permanent's the biggest commitment
a marker can make, so I plan
to take my time with this, only for
polished footsteps
                    to interrupt
the tiled room's pensive acoustics.
Enter two sixth form prefects
lacking in elegance. Just wait,
I almost have it, only a few more
months, but one hops over
the stall to throw the latch open,
jostling me outside. My Head
of Year has sent them, convinced
my life is in danger and I try
to explain to her that, Yes
of course it is; it's a fact
if I can't get this right, I'll simply die.

Monochrome

With less expected, I stay home, leave the house
intermittently: high hopes
to photograph gravestones
or tree tops, chimney pots
with crowned edges, but this childhood town
looks different. The streets are a low
trickle, with everyone at school or work.

I've taken a wrong turn, but loath
to ask directions, keep walking, find myself
at the edge of an island of basalt,
volcanic glossy and black.

From here to horizon the water is
totally flat, not one wave to lift it,
as if some gravity has given
up: dust in the teeth of a celestial
cog. Frost settled over the window
of his cognizance. A fifty-watt sun hangs dead

overhead. There's no sound. He looks down
and notices how pale his feet are
against the rock, like spit-out fingernails.
He's forgotten to dress himself again,
still in these grey pyjama bottoms with
the hole below the crotch. The air's
hard as guilt against his naked arms.

Monotone

I've been stockpiling hair spray, growing
my hair. When it's fifty feet long I'll raise
and set it vertical. My progress assessed
against a tape measure. Before long I'll need

more. I've been thinking of logistics.
A scaffold might be necessary for the final
erection, to hold it steady above my head
when I'm reborn at last as an artefact.

For some reason, my vision strikes them
as obsessive. They say it looks
as if I've not been sleeping, which is true,
but nothing to do with the volume
of my hair. It's that monolithic silence
from the garden keeping me awake.

The doctor nods and gives me my medicines.
I hold them in my palm like the future.
Dependent on producer, they're capsules

of pale green and yellow or plain green
like daffodil buds. It's two to be taken

each day, soon I'll start to feel better,
so to speed up the process, I swallow
two fistfuls and lie down in bed.

Monosyllabic

In here, glass is like cash. A shard
from a vase or jar is good to trade.
I sneak a piece of fish bowl in my shoe
heel. When the head nurse asks me
for the truth I say, No, I'm clean,
and think of my pet fish in his cup.
Most kids find a crack in the wall
or a grate they can lift to hide
their stash. Mine is in a hole
at the foot of my quilt. I think
the plan is to hoard till there's
glass to make a full pane out of,
to look through it and catch
sight of the sun in the sky. This
one girl, a teen like me, she's been
in here for a long time. She's stored
so much glass she can build a whole
door to slide back, step through
and walk off site. A bell rings,
a light flares in the hall. When
it's been three hours at least and they
in some way get her back, she screams
so loud a nurse has to pin her to the floor,
with a jab to the side to help her sleep.
I watch this all from the lounge. I sit
in a worn blue chair and sip my warm
not too hot cup of tea. I should move.
If I'm quick, I can find out where
they take her glass while she's out cold.

Monophagous

I've settled on the medium
of glass for my magnum opus,
but there's no time to learn how
to blow hot glass into shape.
You have to understand, art,
it's not about getting really good at stuff.
I've used empty wine bottles—lashed
them together with bandages.

It's said we have at least one
novelty in us: I've tried to tap
into that secretive vein.
It's said too you never forget your first
blackout. The floorboards are cool
and true on my face. Whole hours

or days have vanished and hanging
over me, this sculpture. I guess
I must've transcended. It's huge,
almost life-sized and just
as ugly as I intended.

Monolatry

Who doesn't love a rerun? Who doesn't
love an ugly pet they can rubberneck?
An internet sensation, a mystery.

He thinks he's people. Watch him
ride on a skateboard. Watch him drink

from a glass. I can follow each pointing
finger round the room like a horse on a
chessboard till I'm back to the square

where I started. I'm a king. I can do
what the hell I want. I can throw up

this poster above my bed. I can upturn
the table and scatter the people like seeds.
I can hurdle the safety gate, stumble upstairs
to the landing and fall through the bannister.

Monophobia

I wasn't at the party where someone climbed
up onto the bathroom sill and jumped

onto the driveway. They didn't die. I think
they were driven to the ER—fractured

their ankle. Typical. The one night I stayed
home decanting the excess of my grey
fluids into bottles and beakers and jars.
I could've been the focus of an online video.

I could be walking round in a cast—a magnet
for signatures. No one wants to sign the labels
on my earnest jars: a handwritten list
of contents and arcane warning symbols.

I've a mind to screw the tops off and put them
back into me, if I have to hear the story again.

I have to learn to handle my expression better
listening to anecdotes where I'm not the star.

Monopod

This or some other camera's
with me always, bulk slung from a shoulder
strap or compact as a penknife
in my pocket, ready to snap.

Digital's fine but analogue
means I can germinate redly
in a dark room, a negative
inverted. I have the chance to break
an image's skin—to watch
sense pooling from the opening. But

I've had this issue of family and friends
appearing shaken or out of focus;

refusing studio work is a given,
but I have gotten quite good at taking

pictures of myself. Contact sheets
full of them. Variations on a fixed gaze
at something out of shot.

If you like, I actually have some work on me.
Let me show you. This is me and this is
me as well and this one here was taken
outside our home—something about
the scale of it makes my head swim.

Monosemic

Lately I keep regaining consciousness
in a dimly lit corridor with a torch in my face.

A nurse asks my name and address, says
to write it on a piece of paper. I do

as she asks., but it's wrong. I've ruined
the spelling. I've drawn a grey symbol. It's

vaguely phallic. The nurse shakes her head
and asks me to wait as she checks on the system

to find out where I'm meant to be and
why I'm so far from there. While she's busy

in another room, I try to remember how
to operate my body. I gain some control

of my lower half—enough to escape through
a fire exit. As I push down on the bar,

an alarm starts blaring. I step into the daylight
of an unfamiliar cityscape. The pavement

and my joggers are caked with vomit.
A taxi driver shakes his head
at the question of me going anywhere.

Monolingual

I tick the box marked *Other* and write
in the space *There's a me-shaped statue growing
inside my body*. The admin guy behind the desk
asks if allowances will need to be made

by the staff at the uni. I say, No. Without
thinking first: my brain beams out its default
signal and my tongue is quick to catch
hold of the frequency, to give nasal shape
to the negative. I'll often give

my answer before hearing the question.
Once, when a doctor saw fit to test my reflexes,
he tapped his rubber hammer to my knee
and I kicked myself.

Monophonic

During a lesson on oscillating waveforms
and their use in audio engineering
I ask my tutor how to synthesise
the silence of waiting at the window
for someone who'll never arrive. He says
he's not sure what it is I'm getting at.

I have this dictaphone recording
of a silence that could illustrate
what I mean—I brought it with me
from home. I could play it if he likes?
He says, No. Not right now. Maybe next

time. Later, in halls of residence,
I download this pirated software and
work out how to knit my silence
into an endless loop. It's so total—
with headphones on, nothing else is audible.

People would pay for a sound like this
—a cold glass chamber they could float in.
Studying the ceiling in bed, I feel
like the filament in a bulb—a taut thread
suspended in inertia. It's days at least

or it could be months before
campus security charge through the door.

Monopolylogue

I made myself sick again. It's cyclical. A
child's error: mixing up flower bulbs
with onions, yet here we are after a bad soup.

The doctor asks why I kept spooning
into my mouth when it must have tasted
clearly bitter as he knows those bulbs do.

I shrug. The doctor— not the same one—
recommends finding a hobby to distract
me while resting at Mom and Dad's.

My camera's packed up in the loft so
I take up sleeping through the day, watch
arthouse cinema when everyone else

is asleep. My favourite film was made
before technicolour or desaturated
for reasons of art: there are fifty characters

played by one actor in various stages
of undress. What plot there is
revolves around a tapered edge

like a skinny glass obelisk, or the head
of a needle—there's no consistency of scale.
In English, it's titled *A Sentiment of Self*

and the runtime falls anywhere
from eighteen hours to eighteen months.
I can quote the whole script from memory.

Recuperation means me rethinking ideas
of self-reliance; my underwear's washed.
I eat what I find in the fridge.

Monomyth

It's easier to exist as an aspect
of a bigger unit.
A sloth needs a branch
and a picture needs a nail
to hang on.

All I can offer is a story
plus this clump of daffodils
taken from the park. They looked
so meaningful in the sun.

I pulled them up, root and clod
and everything. I couldn't
find a vase but I put them in
a pint glass with water. I think
they look nice on the sill.

If your work friends come round
for drinks, they might say,
Hey, those flowers are lovely.
And I'll say, That was me. I did that.

Someone on an internet forum said
they're called *narcissi*.
You're busy. I keep it to myself.

Monosaccharide

If I had a job by now, I'd have saved myself
enough money to quit my job and take

a bus to the airport and a plane out to
anywhere. I could sit in a window seat,

watch the grey squares of the city shrink away.
I could drink a white wine out of see-through

plastic. I could sleep through
what's left of the journey. I've heard across the sea

they have mountains with gods at their peaks.
I could pack my hiking boots and head up there.

I'd sleep dreamless and not gnash my teeth.
I'd buy a better toothbrush and start flossing.

I've typed up a list of aspirations in all
caps and tacked the printouts to the wall

above my bed. They exist as concrete
objects now — they won't disappear

when the future's fickle aperture
shrinks to a pinhole.

Monoxide

Entirely by accident, I break
the world record for holding a breath.
A man arrives with his leather bag

to photograph me for the newsletter.
Let's get a nice one that Mom will like,

he says, and then you can do something silly.
I'll never get used to flashbulbs. Blinking away
a starry yellow overlay,

I ask him if a cash prize is given
to world record holders—see that kind
of money would be helpful right now.
He says, No, but put it on your CV.

Oh. Does he think it's something employers
are looking for? He says, Honestly,
no, I can't imagine anyone would want that.

As he's packing lenses and lighting to go,
I ask him what he knows

about the record for the largest
free-standing monolith, specifically
the kind at the end of a garden.
And he's not certain,
but says he sees these awfully
regularly and some of them
are enormous.

Monoculture

For real this time, I leave it all behind.
Dad drives me to the airport and I sleep

across the sea. I can follow a map
to the place where all the people are.

I eat a pre-packed sandwich as I pass
through a temple erected for an emperor.

A black granite sphinx looks down from a
hieroglyphed pedestal with a stone bowl for offerings
or ritual bonfires. I wish I'd attended
my history lessons. I wish I could know

what it was being asked of me. A man
with no shoes on asks for some change,
so I empty my wallet in his hands.

The people here all speak English. I'm meant to
feel I've cracked a riddle, but there's nothing.

The sunlight they have is different,
but the shadows form the same ugly shapes.

On the beach, I sit alone and watch a reptile
make himself look an idiot, trying and failing
to catch a glossy ant on his tongue. In bed

at the tourist hostel, I fake like I'm sleeping
and replay the whole thing in my head.

Monorail

I once got so scared of dawn's sober approach,
resorted to wandering streets for a night that lasted
a year, home somehow the far side
of the train depot, but I'd turned into

this estate and gotten all spun around. In the
airglow, all those grey structures looked
fifty feet tall and identical. Looking back

on that time, I picture a maze misprinted
on the back of a pub kitchen's kids menu:
a tantrum swirl of grey crayon. There's this

question posed by historians of how
best to memorialise a tragic event.
In most of the circles that ask it's accepted
the purpose is not just to build a museum

to be walked around leisurely, holding up
colourful maps and walkie-talkie audio guides.
It should be remembrance of what's lost, yes—

but also an uncomfortable reminder
of what doesn't bear repeating. It should hurt
to occupy that space again. So why

is there a drawer in my wardrobe, chock full
of hideous commemorative t-shirts? My
kitchen cupboards are stacked with souvenir
glassware I'd never want a guest to find.

Monody

Us two sat on one side of a beer garden bench
behind The Bell when you reached
inside your bag to grab a miniature wine

and pulled out a silver blister pack
instead, by accident flinging a lone
loose tablet to the ground: a white

and yellow daffodil sprung up where it landed
between a crumpled beer mat and
an empty baggy — I recognised myself

there in the dirt, promising
I'd watch over the flower, ensure
its growth was guarded from careless footfall,

but once it started wilting, dropping
its crowned head to the earth
like a sexless monk or a drunk

retching in the road, I couldn't stand
to look at it. The way it bowed so earnestly

made me want to run across a beach and
put my foot through the turrets of sand
some kid spent all day building. Please go

easy on me — it was never my intention
to share this with anyone.

Monocracy

I watch the news now
sat on an antique set of weighing scales: metal
cold against my coccyx helps me focus.
This is part of my new routine. I remember

to wear my glasses and shower every day.
Everything is sharper. When the TV cuts

away from the studio, I recognise
an old friend in the live footage, even
behind their balaclava. I should cast
off my bandages and reach out.

A slow mummification is overrated.
It would take only a moment. The shot

freezes on a brick in midair, just before
it connects with a shopfront window.
The speakers either side of my screen
emit the taut silence of a held breath.

Monotheism

My process of growing up is regretting
this religion I established. In every item
of this temple's iconography, I look

so skinny. In some my face is dripping
like smiling wax given in to a flame
and gravity. I no longer believe in one

great truth—a monolith is just this
big thing that happens to be there.
I'm trying to establish better rituals.

I'm trying to come here less.
Frankly, it's creepy: inside a grey lung, wheezy
with dust, and me putting on my costume,

ironing the collars of my shirt and knotting a tie,
as if anyone will be here to take my picture.

Notes and Acknowledgements

The epigraph for this pamphlet is taken from audio interviews with Diane Arbus, which I originally heard in *Masters of Photography (1972)*.

Massive thanks to everyone who read poems in their earlier forms: George Ttouli, Jessica Syposz, Pip Hibbert, Maeve Haughey, Joshua Blackman, James Roome, Kat Payne Ware and Jack Warren.

Andrew McMillan, thank you for your generosity, for reading and blurbing this pamphlet in its almost finished form.

To my friends, near and far, here and gone, close and estranged, I love you all dearly. Likewise my family, who haven't seen these poems yet, but helped me through those rough times that laid their foundations.

Thanks also to Caroline Bird and Roger Robinson, whose kindness and advice continue to make me a better writer and a better person.

Thanks to Aaron Kent and the Broken Sleep Books team who took a chance on me and helped turn things around.

Thanks and love always to Katie, who I couldn't do any of this without.

And finally, my love to you, reading this. I hope these poems find you well.

LAY OUT YOUR UNREST